A TRUE BOOK™

# South America

## LIBBY KOPONEN

Children's Press®
An Imprint of Scholastic Inc.
New York   Toronto   London   Auckland   Sydney
Mexico City   New Delhi   Hong Kong
Danbury, Connecticut

**Content Consultant**

Hannah H. Covert
Executive Director
Center for Latin American Studies
University of Florida
Gainesville, FL

Library of Congress Cataloging-in-Publication Data

Koponen, Libby.
  South America / by Libby Koponen.
       p. cm. -- (A true book)
  Includes index.
     ISBN-13: 978-0-531-16869-1  (lib. bdg.)
              978-0-531-21831-0  (pbk.)
     ISBN-10: 0-531-16869-7  (lib. bdg.)
              0-531-21831-7  (pbk.)

1.  South America--Juvenile literature.  I. Title.

  F2208.5.K67 2008
  980--dc22                    2007048088

Produced by Weldon Owen Education Inc.

1 2 3 4 5 6 7 8 9 10 R 18 17 16 15 14 13 12 11 10 09

# Find the Truth!

**Everything** you are about to read is true *except* for one of the sentences on this page.

Which one is **TRUE**?

T or F   The Atacama Desert in Chile reaches only 75°F (24°C), at its hottest.

T or F   The Andes is the highest mountain range in the world.

Find the answers in this book.

3

# Contents

**THE BIG TRUTH!**

## Floating Village

Potatoes were first grown in South America.

# **4** Lifestyles

Angel Falls, in Venezuela, is named for American pilot Jimmy Angel. He saw the falls in 1933 and told the world about them.

# CHAPTER 1

# Land of Extremes

South America boasts the world's driest desert, tallest waterfall, longest mountain range, largest rain forest, and biggest river by volume of flow. Yet it is only the fourth-largest continent. It is made up of 12 independent countries and three territories. It has huge cities as well as vast stretches of wilderness.

Angel Falls is the world's tallest waterfall. It is almost 20 times higher than Niagara Falls.

La Paz, in the Bolivian Andes, is the world's highest capital city.

## On Top of the World

South America makes up one-eighth of Earth's land. The Andes (AN-deez) Mountains run down its entire western side. At 4,500 miles (7,242 kilometers), the Andes range is the world's longest. The highest peaks rise to more than 20,000 feet (6,096 meters). The Himalayas in Asia are higher, but the Andes are still growing! One of Earth's **tectonic plates** is sliding under the one next to it. This overlapping movement pushes the Andes upward.

Caribbean Sea

South America

Galápagos
Islands
(Ecuador)

Venezuela

Guyana

Suriname

French Guiana
(France)

Andes Mountains

Llanos

Guiana Highlands

Colombia

Angel Falls

Equator

Ecuador

Amazon River

Peru

Amazon
Basin

Brazil

Lake Titicaca

Brazilian
Highlands

South Pacific Ocean

Bolivia

Martin Vaz
Islands
(Brazil)

Gran
Chaco

Atacama Desert

Paraguay

Iguaçu
Falls

Juan Fernández
Islands
(Chile)

Pampas

Uruguay

South Atlantic Ocean

Argentina

Chile

Andes Mountains

N

W        E

S

Falkland Islands
(U.K.)

South Georgia
Island
(U.K.)

Cape Horn

9

Scarlet ibis, snowy egrets, and other wading birds thrive in the wetlands of the Llanos, or plains, of Venezuela.

# Swamp Site

East of the Andes, in eastern Colombia and western Venezuela, are the Llanos (YA-nos). These are grassy, treeless plains. They are swampy in the wet season and dusty in the dry season. Wildlife is varied. There are hundreds of **species** of birds. There are also crocodiles, anacondas, freshwater dolphins, **capybaras**, armadillos, giant turtles, piranhas, and giant anteaters.

## Tall Tables

In the north of South America are the Guiana Highlands. The area takes up parts of Venezuela, Guyana, Suriname, French Guiana, and Brazil. The highlands feature massive sandstone **mesas**. These tabletop mountains are called tepui (tey-POO-ee). There are more than a hundred of them in Venezuela. Angel Falls cascades over the cliff of a tepui.

The word *tepui* means "house of the gods."

Tepuis are some of the oldest rock formations in the world.

# Plenty of Plains

In the middle of the continent are grassy lowlands. The Gran Chaco (grahn CHAH-koh) is hot and dry. It covers parts of Argentina, Paraguay, and Bolivia. A tree called the quebracho (keh-BRAH-choh) grows there. Quebrachos provide strong timber, and **tannin** for dyeing leather.

South of the Gran Chaco are the Pampas. These flat, **fertile** plains extend into Argentina, Paraguay, Uruguay, and Brazil. The Pampas support crops, such as soybeans, corn, and wheat. There are also many cattle ranches.

**Cowboys on the Pampas are called *gauchos* (GOU-chohs).**

**Moon Valley in the Atacama Desert has dramatic rock formations.**

## Desert Dunes

The Atacama Desert in Chile is made up of sand, dry salt beds, and lava flows. One area has geysers and hot springs. Temperatures in the desert range between 32°F and 75°F (0°C and 24°C).

The sky above the Atacama is extremely clear. It is one of the best places in the world for studying the stars. This is because the Atacama is Earth's driest desert. Its average annual rainfall is less than half an inch (1.27 centimeters).

Visitors to Iguaçu Falls can view them from below in a small boat.

# Wild Waters

Iguaçu (ee-gwah-SOO) Falls is on the border of Brazil and Argentina. Iguaçu is actually 275 falls that extend along 1.67 miles (2.7 kilometers) of the Iguaçu River. The falls range in height from 130 feet to 270 feet (40 meters to 82 meters). They are surrounded by national parks. The falls region is known for its diverse plant life. It is also home to hundreds of kinds of butterflies.

# Cruising the Coast

South America's coastlines are varied. On the east coast, tourists crowd the white-sand beaches. On the west coast, some beaches have volcanic black sand. Ecuador's Pacific coast has a fertile plain with enormous banana plantations. Chile has rugged terrain and wild seas. Southern Chile also has thousands of small coastal islands.

La Portada is a giant sandstone arch off the coast of northern Chile. In the arch and cliffs are fossils that are millions of years old.

# Extreme Exploring

The region at the southern tip of South America is called Patagonia (pat-uh-GOH-nee-uh). It is mostly in Argentina. Patagonia's landscape includes the Andes in the west and dry **plateaus** and plains to the east. Because of the wind and cold, few people live in Patagonia. However, it is popular with hikers. Visitors to the coast see penguins, sea lions, and whales. There are also gigantic **glaciers** that move slowly down to the sea.

Some people explore Patagonia in kayaks to view the glaciers up close.

# Island Life

**Blue-footed booby**

The Galápagos (ga-LA-pa-gohs) Islands lie about 600 miles (966 kilometers) west of Ecuador. The 19 volcanic islands cover an area of 3,029 square miles (7,844 square kilometers).

Galápagos wildlife is remarkable. The penguins there live farther north than any other kind. The islands' marine iguana is the only lizard that feeds in the ocean. One kind of diving bird has huge, bright-blue feet. There are tortoises weighing more than 500 pounds (227 kilograms). Today, the Galápagos Islands are a nature preserve.

**Marine iguana**

Tiny poison-dart frogs come in many colors. Their skin is covered with poison. Hunters in the Amazon use the poison on the tips of blowgun darts.

# CHAPTER 2

# Amazing Amazon

South America is home to both one of the driest places on Earth *and* one of the wettest! The Amazon rain forest is the world's largest **tropical** rain forest. It covers about two million square miles (5.2 million square kilometers), mostly in Brazil. The Amazon River carries more water than any other river. Only the Nile in Egypt is longer.

The toucan's call sounds like a croaking frog.

# Home to Millions

The Amazon rain forest is hot and humid. It receives about nine feet of rain every year. The average temperature is 80°F (27°C). Plants and animals thrive in this environment. Some trees grow to be over 165 feet (50 meters) tall. There are more different species there than in all the rest of the world.

**Tapirs live in the Amazon. They are related to horses and rhinoceroses.**

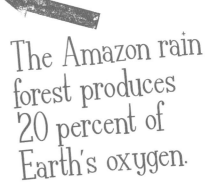

The Amazon rain forest produces 20 percent of Earth's oxygen.

# Protecting the Forest

The Amazon rain forest is in danger. Many parts of it have been cleared for ranching, logging, and farming. This takes away places where plants and animals can live. **Indigenous** people fish, hunt, and harvest rubber, fruits, nuts, and oils from the forest. They also raise and collect medicinal plants.

The government of Brazil has now recognized that **sustainable** use of the forest makes sense. It has set up protected reserves managed by indigenous communities. The forest has been given a chance to recover and survive.

Rubber trees are cut on an angle to let the sap flow. One tree can produce sap for about five years.

21

# Floating Village

Lake Titicaca (tee-tee-KAH-kah) is located on the border of Peru and Bolivia. It is the highest navigable lake in the world. It is also home to the Uro-Aymara Indians. They actually live *on* the water! They construct floating islands from reeds that grow on the shore. The Uro-Aymara also build their houses and boats from these reeds.

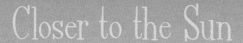

## Closer to the Sun

**Lake Titicaca lies 12,507 feet (3,812 meters) above sea level. At that elevation, the sunlight, wind, and cold can be extreme. The Uro-Aymara wear several layers of clothing to protect themselves.**

## Survival Tactics

**Fresh reeds must be laid down daily to keep the islands from sinking. For cooking, villagers build fires on a layer of rocks. This keeps the reeds from catching fire.**

The centuries-old Inca Festival of the Sun takes place each year on June 24.

# CHAPTER 3

# Peoples of the Past

In southern Chile, there are ruins from about 10,500 B.C. They are remains of the earliest known human settlement in South America. Some scientists believe that the people who lived there walked down from North America. Others think that they arrived in boats from Asia or Africa. By 1500 A.D., about 30 million people lived on the continent.

The Inca called gold "the sweat of the sun" and silver "the tears of the moon."

# Mountain Dwellers

The Andes were home to many indigenous groups. Their descendants continue to live there today.

One group, the Chibcha (CHIB-chuh), lived in the northern Andes, in what is now Colombia. The Chibcha buried important people as mummies. Finely worked gold objects were often buried with them. One Chibcha legend tells of El Dorado — "the Golden One." In the story, the king was coated with gold dust. He was put on a raft filled with gold treasures and rowed to an island. There, he dived into the lake, washing away the gold dust. The treasure was thrown in after him.

In the 1530s, the Spanish explorers arrived. They had heard of the legend and searched for the gold. They took gold from many people, but they never found El Dorado's treasure.

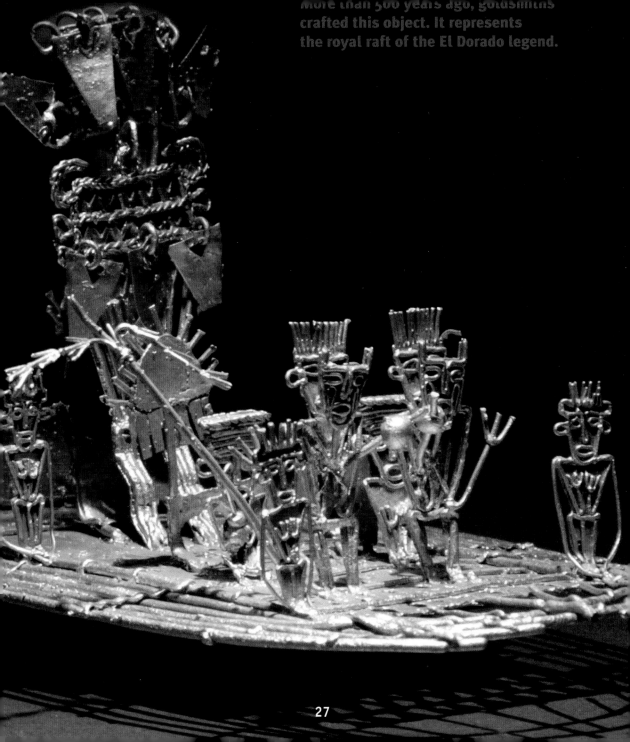

More than 500 years ago, goldsmiths
crafted this object. It represents
the royal raft of the El Dorado legend.

## Large and in Charge

The earliest Inca lived in the area of Cusco (KOOS-koh), Peru, beginning in about 1200. By 1532, Inca lands extended most of the length of the Andes Mountains. By the late 1530s, Spain had taken control of the Inca empire. However, Quechua (KEH-chwa), the Inca language, survived. Today, it is the most widely spoken indigenous language in the Americas.

Inca Empire 1532

Colombia

Ecuador

Peru

Brazil

Machu Picchu

Cusco

Bolivia

Chile

Argentina

At the height of its power, the Inca empire numbered about 10 million people.

28

The Inca were skilled engineers. They built thousands of miles of roads. They made suspension bridges of grass rope across rivers and canyons. Ruins of Inca buildings show stone walls perfectly fitted together without cement.

Machu Picchu (mah-choo PEEK-choo) is an ancient Inca city in the Peruvian Andes. Its residents abandoned the city in the 1530s. In 1911, it was rediscovered by an American explorer.

**Machu Picchu is thought to have been a home of the Inca royal family.**

# Caribbean Conquests

The main groups that lived along the Caribbean coast of South America were the Arawak (AR-uh-wak) and the Carib (ka-RIB). In 1498, explorer Christopher Columbus landed on the coast. He was the first European to arrive. Diseases brought by the Europeans wiped out many of the indigenous people. Others were killed in battle. Beginning in the 1600s, the Dutch and then the British claimed coastal areas. These areas are now the independent countries of Suriname and Guyana.

## South America Time Line

**About 10,500 B.C.**
People live in Monte Verde, Chile. They use stone tools and preserve plants.

**1530s**
Spanish explorers invade South America.

# Priestly Protection

In the early 1600s, Catholic priests went to South America to convert native people to Christianity. They gathered the Guaraní (gwah-rah-NEE) people into settlements at Catholic missions. There the Guaraní grew their food, made their clothes, and learned to read and write. The priests protected the Guaraní against slave traders until 1767. In that year, the priests had to leave the region. The settlements declined and the Guaraní survived on their own again. Today, Guaraní is an official language of Paraguay.

## 1500s–1800s

Europeans take Africans to South America to work as slaves.

## 1888

Slavery ends in Brazil. Millions of people from all over the world begin moving to South America.

# The Undefeated

The southern end of South America was originally home to the Mapuche (ma-POO-cheh) people. Neither the Inca nor the Spanish were able to conquer them. In 1641, after a century of fighting, the Spanish signed a treaty recognizing Mapuche territory. However, Chile and Argentina are now independent nations. Today, the Mapuche are struggling to retain control of their lands.

The Mapuche in Chile still perform traditional ceremonies.

**Thousands of Africans were brought to Brazil. They were forced to work as slaves in mines and on coffee and sugar plantations.**

# Brazil Is Born

The area that is now Brazil was once inhabited by as many as 2,000 indigenous groups. In 1500, Portuguese explorer Pedro Álvares Cabral landed on the east coast of South America. He claimed the land for Portugal. Indigenous people died out in huge numbers. Some were absorbed into the colonial population. Portugal ruled Brazil until 1822. Portuguese is still Brazil's official language.

# CHAPTER 4

# Lifestyles

In South America today, some people have high standards of living, while millions of others live in poverty. Most countries struggle to expand economically in a way that improves the lives of the poor as well as the wealthy. The most developed economies on the continent are those of Brazil, Argentina, Colombia, and Chile.

Soccer is the most popular sport in South America.

# Living off the Land

About a third of South America's land is used for farming or ranching. The biggest **exports** are beef, wool, coffee, sugar, bananas, grains, and soybeans. Even high in the Andes, the land is used. Like the ancient Inca, farmers there grow crops such as corn and potatoes on terraced hillsides. Some people in the mountains raise llamas and alpacas for wool.

Peoples of the Andes weave colorful clothing and blankets with alpaca wool.

Most of the world's emeralds come from Colombia.

## Mining for Money

Mining is a profitable industry in South America. The continent has massive reserves of oil, natural gas, gold, coal, iron ore, and other valuable minerals. Atacama Desert is rich in copper and in sodium nitrate. Sodium nitrate is used to make fertilizer and gunpowder.

# Colorful Cultures

Brazil is home to many ethnic groups. São Paulo, South America's biggest city, has the largest Japanese population outside of Japan. A mix of Portuguese and African styles is typical of Brazil's music and its food. The popular arts reflect the European, Asian, African, and indigenous people who make up Brazil today.

**Capoeira (ka-poh-AIR-uh) is a dance form and a martial art. It was developed during the 1500s by enslaved Africans brought to Brazil.**

Santiago's sleek subway features towering murals.

# Modern Transport

Santiago, the capital of Chile, is a large, modern city. It is one of the main financial centers in South America. The city is surrounded by the Andes Mountains. To help reduce its high level of air pollution, Santiago has a public subway system. The *Metro de Santiago* carries more than two million passengers a day. It is one of the cleanest and safest subways in the world.

# "Paris of the South"

Buenos Aires (BWEH-nohs EYE-ress) is the capital of Argentina. It lies on the eastern edge of the Pampas, on a river called Río de la Plata.

**Immigrants** from Italy and Spain have lent Buenos Aires a European flavor. The city has an opera house, many museums and cinemas, and countless cafés and restaurants. It has large plazas and parks. The *Avenida 9 de Julio* is the world's widest boulevard. For its special style, Buenos Aires is sometimes called the "Paris of the South."

**Tango began in Buenos Aires in the early 1900s. It is a popular music and dance form worldwide.**

# Great Painting

La Boca in Buenos Aires was once a community of immigrants. People built their houses from metal scraps. They painted them in whatever paint they could find. The neighborhood was a hodgepodge. It was also home to a boy named Benito Quinquela Martín. He grew up to be a successful painter. He bought a block of La Boca's run-down buildings. He started a children's art school. The community helped repaint the buildings in bright colors. Today, La Boca is the most colorful neighborhood in Buenos Aires.

# Religion

The majority of people in South America are Catholic. Early Spanish and Portuguese explorers converted many indigenous people. Some people of indigenous or African ancestry combine Catholicism with their traditional spiritual beliefs. Recently, Protestant religions have become more common on the continent. As with other aspects of life in South America, religion shows the influences of indigenous, African, European, and Asian cultures. ★

**Many festivals in South America involve parades with masks and costumed dancers.**

# True Statistics

**Population of South America:** About 371 million
**Percentage of world's population:** About 6
**Largest city in South America:** São Paulo, Brazil (More than 18 million people)
**Size of South America:** 6,898,000 square miles (17,866,000 square kilometers)
**Percentage of world's land:** About 12
**Size of Brazil:** 3,300,171 square miles (8,547,403 square kilometers)—bigger than the 48 contiguous states of the United States
**Length of Amazon River:** 4,000 miles (6,437 kilometers)
**Height of Angel Falls:** 3,212 feet (979 meters)

## Did you find the truth?

**T** The Atacama Desert in Chile reaches only 75°F (24°C), at its hottest.

**F** The Andes is the highest mountain range in the world.

# Resources

## Books

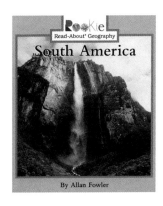

Aloian, Molly and Kalman, Bobbie. *Explore South America* (Explore the Continents). New York: Crabtree Publishing Company, 2007.

Eagen, James. *The Aymara of South America* (First Peoples). Minneapolis: Lerner Publishing Group, 2002.

Fowler, Allan. *South America* (Rookie Read-About Geography). Danbury, CT: Children's Press, 2001.

Freedman, Russell. *Who Was First?: Discovering the Americas*. New York: Clarion Books, 2007.

Ganeri, Anita. *Living in the Amazon Rain Forest* (World Cultures). Chicago: Raintree, 2007.

Gruber, Beth. *Ancient Inca: Archaeology Unlocks the Secrets of Inca's Past* (National Geographic Investigates). Washington, DC: National Geographic Children's Books, 2006.

Hynson, Colin. *You Wouldn't Want to Be an Inca Mummy!: A One-Way Journey You'd Rather Not Make*. Danbury, CT: Franklin Watts, 2007.

Somervill, Barbara A. *The Land of the Andes* (Geography of the World). Mankato, MN: The Child's World, 2004.

# Organizations and Web Sites

### Minnesota State University
www.mnsu.edu/emuseum/prehistory/latinamerica/
index.shtml
Read about ancient sites and people in South America.

### National Geographic
www.nationalgeographic.com/ngkids/games/brainteaser/
inca/inca.html
Play an Inca game and learn about mummies and other secrets
of the Inca.

### Amazon Interactive
www.eduweb.com/amazon.html
Find out what life is really like in the Ecuadorian Amazon.

# Places to Visit

### Iguaçu Falls
Rodovia BR 469
KM 18, Foz do Iguaçu
Paraná, Brasil
+55 (45) 3521 4400
www.cataratasdoiguacu.com.
br/cataratas_en.asp
Visit these amazing falls
and see the colorful wildlife.

### Wax Museum
Dr. Enrique del Valle Iberlucea,
1261, La Boca
Buenos Aires, Argentina
+54 (11) 4303 0563
www.museodecera.com.ar/
menu.htm
View lifelike figures showing
scenes from La Boca's history.

# Important Words

**capybara** (kap-uh-BAHR-uh) – a large South American rodent that lives along the banks of rivers and lakes

**exports** – goods sent to another country to be sold there

**fertile** (FUR-tuhl) – able to produce crops

**glacier** – a large mass of slow-moving ice

**immigrant** (IM-i-grunht) – a person who comes from abroad to live permanently in a country

**indigenous** (in-DIJ-uh-nuhss) – relating to the original people living in an area

**mesa** – a land formation having steep walls and a flat top. *Mesa* means "table" in Spanish.

**navigable** (NAV-i-guh-bul) – able to be sailed on by boats and ships

**plateau** (pla-TOH) – an area of high, flat land

**species** (SPEE-sheez) – a group of plants or animals that share common characteristics and are able to reproduce

**sustainable** (suh-STAIN-uh-buhl) – able to be continued without long-term negative effect on the environment

**tannin** – a natural substance used for dyeing leather

**tectonic plate** – one of the large slabs of rock that make up Earth's outer crust

**tropical** – to do with the hot areas of Earth near the equator

# Index

Page numbers in **bold** indicate illustrations

# About the Author

Libby Koponen is the author of *North America*, another True Book, and *Blow Out the Moon*, a novel based on a true story about an American girl who goes to an English boarding school. Libby has a B.A. in history from Wheaton College and an M.F.A. in writing from Brown University. She has traveled all over the world and ridden horses on every continent except Antarctica. She lives in Mystic, CT.

**PHOTOGRAPHS**: Big Stock Photo (© Eric Isselée, back cover; blue-footed booby, p. 17; p. 20; p. 29); Getty Images (front cover; p. 11; p. 32; p. 34); istockphoto.com (p. 4; p. 14; p. 16; p. 19; p. 30; ship, p. 31; p. 37; p. 41; p. 43); Photolibrary (potatoes, p. 5; p. 6; p. 8; p. 10; pp. 12–13; p. 15; marine iguana, p. 17; p. 18; pp. 21–24; p. 33; p. 38); Stock.XCHNG (p. 40); Tranz: Corbis (woman, p. 5; p. 39; p. 42; Reuters, p. 27); Victor Englebert (p. 36)